INTRODUCTION

WRITING IS HARD WORK,
BUT MAYBE IT DOESN'T HAVE TO BE.

Whether you're an aspiring novelist, an avid journaler, or someone who simply loves to communicate through the written word, the only thing that makes writing easier is more writing, which is to say, simply writing more.

The more we write, the more we learn from our mistakes and our experiments. We push ourselves, we mess up, we try again, we make discoveries, and we savor our successes. The prompts in this yearlong diary are designed to help you challenge yourself as a writer no matter what your end goal might be. *Q&A a Day for Writers* provides page after page of inspiring quotes from famous writers to use as jumping-off points, thought experiments, and personal questions that will help you harness and assess your own desires. As Ray Bradbury said of the act of writing, "You are in the midst of a moving process." Let this diary be a simple and inspiring record of that wondrous and very personal process.

Copyright © 2016 by Clarkson Potter/Publishers,
an imprint of the Crown Publishing Group,
a division of Penguin Random House LLC.
All rights reserved.

Published in the United States by Clarkson Potter/
Publishers, an imprint of the Crown Publishing Group,
a division of Penguin Random House LLC, New York.
crownpublishing.com
clarksonpotter.com

CLARKSON POTTER is a trademark and POTTER
with colophon is a registered trademark of Penguin
Random House LLC.

Library of Congress Cataloging-in-Publication Data is
available upon request.

ISBN 978-0-451-49490-0

Printed in China

TEXT BY Chelsea Holden Baker DeLorme
BOOK AND COVER DESIGN BY Danielle Deschenes
COVER ILLUSTRATION © shutterstock.com / Bloomua

10 9 8 7 6 5 4 3 2 1

First Edition

1/1/19

This was a difficult day. Bella Mestram slept over for New Years and we all stayed up watching The Taylor Swift concert and then random musical interludes on TV until finally it was midnight. I was in a lot of pain all day, Holly, Layla, Gwen, Lisa, Bella and Olivia went bowling, the kids slept over at Stella and Jasper's house, I curled up on the couch and watched "Philip K Dick's Electric Dreams."

In her essay "Fail Better," Zadie Smith says, "The very reason I write is so that I might not sleepwalk through my entire life." Why do *you* write? What does it do for you?

1/4/19

2

Studies have shown
that thousands of
personality traits
can be linked to
handwriting. For
example, crowded
letters indicate
a person who has no
concern for personal
space. Use a hand-
writing sample to
inspire a character
sketch.

Another day on the couch.
The boys slept over at Bella,
Nico and Sara, Holly spent
most of the day then too and
I watched on the couch.

Maybe this day
for Stella/Super
Sleepover.

1/3/19

Can you summon
what you believe
to be your earliest
memory? Why
do you think you
remembered that
of all things?

I actually worked from home some on this day, laying on the couch and holding my laptop over my head. Participating in video meetings. At 1:00 Dad came over to drive me to the hospital. I had to use a wheelchair to get checked in. A little old Vietnamese woman was my nurse. She told me she would pray for me as she wheeled me to the x-ray room. I had to lay on my stomach for the epidural shot. They shoved pillows underneath me to relieve the pain but it did not work. The doctor remarked that my back muscles were spasming as he inserted the needle. Not too bad at first but when he shoved it in deeper, puncturing something, I whimpered into my pillow. Eventually it was over. It helped a small bit. The nurse was pleased. Dad drove me home and I was back to feeling sick.

Maybe they slept at Nico, Bela's this day?

4

The wind whipped up and the hillside raised its hackles. Can you come up with a few descriptions that ascribe an animalistic quality to something that doesn't breathe?

Felt a little better this day. The boil + Holly went to the Bell museum, I worked from home and was able to sit up most of the day. I took a shower while

everyone was gone but it was very difficult and I was nervous that I was going to fall or otherwise hurt myself. I am listening through a bunch of my records and started reading "Death's End" third book in the "Three-body" trilogy by Cixin Liu.

This is the first day of the year that I've felt relatively like myself again. Holly and the kids just left to go roller-skating. Layla will be using the new skates she got for Christmas. They all went to their respective dance/ehrink classes, this afternoon they came back home. Holly took Pixie for a walk and the kids stayed at home with me. It was the first time since I hurt my back on the 26th that I've been able to snuggle and read to Sam. I could tell that he had missed it as much as I had. Layla wore her David Bowie shirt for the first time and we used some of the hair markers that Chris gave her for Christmas to put a tiny green streak in both her and Sam's hair. Eventually Holly came home with Pixie, and the kids spent some time riling her up before they had to go, and, not Mat and Mike at the roller rink, listening to the Transporting soundtrack and feeling lucky.

Select a family photo, then write about the things you *can't* see in the picture.

JANUARY

6

Using the same photo
from yesterday,
describe the people
in the picture as if
you're seeing them
for the first time.

Think over the
past week. What
was the strangest or
funniest thing you
witnessed?

JANUARY

8

Every scar tells a story. Write the story of a scar you know well—yours or someone else's.

Someone* once said, "Writing about music is like dancing about architecture." Try it anyway.

(*There is more than one apocryphal story of where this quote came from.)

JANUARY

10

The word *set* has over 440 different uses in the English language. Challenge yourself to fill this space using *set* in as many ways as possible.

11

How would your
friends describe you
to a stranger?

_____

_____

_____

_____

_____

_____

_____

_____

_____

_____

_____

_____

_____

_____

_____

_____

_____

_____

_____

_____

_____

_____

_____

_____

_____

A first lady is sometimes referred to as an éminence grise when she uses her position of influence to affect policy without an official title. Create an éminence grise character who could powerfully, but quietly, shift the plotline of a novel.

Writers from Stephen King to William Faulkner have stressed the connection between being a good reader and being a good writer. Spend a few moments writing about a book that inspires you.

JANUARY

14

Think of a person
and describe his
or her personality
through writing
about a cup they
often drink from
(real or imagined).

15

In Thomas Pynchon's book *Bleeding Edge*, a character says, "Paranoia's the garlic in life's kitchen . . . you can never have too much." Use an element of your own paranoia to spark a story.

JANUARY

16

Write a description of
"the offing," the most
distant extent of the
sea that can be seen
from the shore.

If you had to build
a diorama that
represented your
interior world, what
would people see
when peering inside?

JANUARY

18

Stendhal Syndrome, sometimes also called hyperkulturemia or Florence Syndrome (the city where Stendhal himself first swooned), is the psychosomatic disorder of being physically overwhelmed by art and tends to overtake tourists in cities highly saturated with museums and public artwork, especially when the traveler doesn't speak the language. Put yourself in the shoes of a tourist in Paris, experiencing its thrall.

Think of a scenario
that you would find
deeply uncomfortable.
Now write about it as
someone else.

20

Pick a place—
it doesn't have to
be a cold place—
and describe the
first snowfall of
the year there.

Filmmaker Joss Whedon once said, "Time travel is a concept that has been done and so is every other thing you will ever think of. So the thing that makes it worth saying is only going to be you." What are the opening lines in your time travel film?

JANUARY

22

Have you ever had a
visceral reaction to
blood or sickness?
Use those feelings
and sensations in a
short anecdote.

23

Describe a memorable
person you met just
once and will likely
never see again.

JANUARY

24

In an alternate
universe where there
are no consequences
to you, what kind
of revenge would
you mete out,
and on whom?

25

Think of classic characters whose hair held great power (e.g., Lady Godiva, Rapunzel, Samson). Who would be your hero in a modern story of someone with long, potent locks?

JANUARY

26

Think about the
most enjoyable
moment you had
alone recently.
Why was that time
meaningful or
necessary for you?

I'm sitting in the dark now. light The snow is piling down outside. The streetlight right where my bedroom illuminates the snow that falls with a strange somewhat foreign light. I've been on the couch for a month now. I'm listening to a drone record called "Tecumseh". Sam and Lyla are in bed and Holly is nesting in the bath. Andy and Bill will come to shovel or snowblow tomorrow morning. Andy said he'll be here at 6:00 8-12 inches of snow but it -15 on Wednesday. I can move about a little better now. I am still afraid to do much more than sit around the house. My leg still hurts some but I am amazed by how painful it was a few weeks ago. It was the worst pain I've ever experienced.

Tecumseh - Avalanche and Inundation good "Blizzard Music"

Take a drone's-eye view of your neighborhood (Google Earth can help with details if you need them) to imagine what a spaceship might see when it's landing.

JANUARY

28

You're in a car
traveling 100 mph.
Does this exhilarate
or frighten you?
Who is driving?
Where are you going?

Visualize this:
a sphere beneath
a tree. What do
you see?

JANUARY

30

Look up the Portuguese/Galician word *saudade*. A rare word that has no equivalent in other languages, it is a cousin of *nostalgia*, but it captures a stronger melancholy that comes from knowing you are not likely to again experience the thing you long for, although you will carry the memory or idea with you always. After you read more about it, write about your own feeling(s) of *saudade* here.

JANUARY

31

Elmore Leonard famously advised not to start a novel with a description of the weather. Break that rule and write about today's weather.

FEBRUARY

1

What are your
top five goals, as a
writer and/or for
your writing in the
coming months?

2

Curse a character
with kleptomania.
What is he or she
taking and why?

FEBRUARY

3

Shakespeare is credited with inventing words, such as *advertising, moonbeam, undress, assassination, blanket, amazement, lackluster, madcap, critic,* and *puking.* Select a few of these words to write into a passage here.

4

Quitting often has a
negative connotation.
Flip that idea on its
head and recall
(or imagine) the
sweet freedom
that can come from
a cut-and-run.

FEBRUARY

5

Attempt to fill
this space with a
short story that
employs only single-
syllable words.
You could begin:
"The last time I
saw her . . ."

6

Graphic designer James Victore likes to remind people that "the things that make you weird as a kid will make you great tomorrow." What does this mean for you?

FEBRUARY

7

Close your eyes
and imagine
unexpectedly
coming face to face
with an animal—
any animal. Now
imagine that
you're the animal,
and write from
there.

FEBRUARY

8

Think of a favorite
food and describe it
only through texture.

_____

_____

_____

_____

_____

_____

_____

_____

_____

_____

_____

_____

_____

_____

_____

_____

_____

_____

_____

_____

_____

_____

_____

_____

_____

_____

_____

FEBRUARY

9

Record the last thing
you were thinking
about in the shower,
no matter how
dreamy or mundane.

It is said that the cure for grief is motion. Recount an activity that has propelled you through sadness.

11

Find a way to
use MacGyver as
a verb in a story
involving only
mundane objects.

12

Have you ever attempted a homolinguistic translation? "Translate" a favorite short poem, English to English. Substitute words with synonyms, similar phrases, or just by capturing the general sense of a line until an entirely unique poem emerges.

13

Continue this story:
"For once the fulgent
sun was not a
welcome sight . . ."

Erika Eiffel took her surname after her 2007 marriage to the Eiffel Tower. Begin a short story about someone in love with an inanimate object or structure here.

FEBRUARY

15

Norman Mailer claimed that "insomnia is the mind's revenge for all the thoughts we forgot to have in the day." What do you think about when you can't sleep?

When have you
experienced
euphoria, and
how would you
describe it?

FEBRUARY

17

Design a scene
where tranquility
is unnerving. What
makes it eerie?
Can you impart the
feeling without
using the words
unnerving, eerie, or
their synonyms?

Edgar Allan Poe's masterwork "The Raven" makes use of assonance, the repetition of vowel sounds: "Ah, distinctly I remember it was in the bleak December / And each separate dying ember wrought its ghost upon the floor." (Note the "ur" sound.) Long vowel sounds can slow down a line, creating a more serious mood; short vowel sounds can increase energy and levity. Play with this technique in a few trial lines of your own.

19

Open yourself up to
all geographies and
time periods and
imagine a society
with an unusual
currency—it is
not paper, gold, or
bitcoin. What is it,
and where does it
come from?

The Bible shows up in great works of art, literature, and music time and time again. Find a common phrase that comes from the Bible (such as "wit's end," "to everything there is a season," or "the blind leading the blind") to inspire today's entry.

FEBRUARY

21

Imagine your dream
house: What does
the front door look
like? Can you detail
the whole entryway?

Famous last words: consider the last sentences of one of your favorite books. Now write your own "last sentence" to an as yet unwritten novel.

23

Continue this story:
"It was never
supposed to be
this way . . ."

FEBRUARY

24

Busyness often feels like a modern affliction. Cast yourself into any era of the past and take up the life of a busy person then. What consumes you? What overwhelms you? What do you wish you could get away from?

FEBRUARY

25

Attempt to make
a logic puzzle or
rebus with words.
Here's an example:
PAWALKRK.
Can you figure it out?

Have you ever seen
a pair of sneakers
with their laces
tied, thrown over
a telephone wire?
Write a backstory
for these kicks—
how did they get
there?

27

Pick a number between one and twelve. Got it? Now write every association you have with that number.

28

Inhabit a moment
of fear you had as a
child and write it out.

_____

_____

_____

_____

_____

_____

_____

_____

_____

_____

_____

_____

_____

_____

_____

_____

_____

_____

_____

_____

_____

_____

_____

_____

_____

FEBRUARY
29

LEAP YEAR ONLY

Describe the greatest
leap you've ever taken.

MARCH

1

John Barth once remarked: "My feeling about technique in art is that it has about the same value as technique in lovemaking. That is to say, heartfelt ineptitude has its appeal and so does heartless skill; but what you want is passionate virtuosity." Use this space for a freewrite.

MARCH

2

You're visiting a
new friend's house
for the first time,
and they're making
dinner. You find
yourself alone in the
kitchen and lift the
lid off the pot on
the stove. To your
horror, _____
is inside. Fill in the
blank and the rest
of the scene.

Picture yourself on
a path in the woods.
Now something
appears. Describe
it all.

4

Write an apology
as a short poem.

Try to place yourself
at the moment of a
baby's birth. Focus
on the emotions in
the room during a
calm birth, or create
a scene of dramatic
arrival.

MARCH

6

An authority figure
is drenched in water.
What just happened?

7

Thomas Edison liked to use hypnagogia— the liminal state between wakefulness and sleep—to his benefit by dozing in a chair with a bottle in his hand. When his muscles relaxed (the transition from lucid dreaming to sleep), the bottle would thump to the floor, waking him up to take advantage of thoughts that would have otherwise escaped him. Try it and record the experience.

8

Let's take a spin through the Seven Deadly Sins. Write what comes to mind after each prompt. Today: an eighty-year-old woman shocked by her own lust.

Let's take a spin
through the Seven
Deadly Sins. Write
what comes to mind
after each prompt.
Today: a woman
petrified by gluttony.

10

Let's take a spin
through the Seven
Deadly Sins. Write
what comes to mind
after each prompt.
Today: a ten-year-
old awakening
to his greed.

Let's take a spin
through the Seven
Deadly Sins. Write
what comes to mind
after each prompt.
Today: a day trader
with secret sloth.

12

Let's take a spin
through the Seven
Deadly Sins. Write
what comes to mind
after each prompt.
Today: a quiet
bookstore clerk who
is hired for "wrath
channeling" on
the side.

Let's take a spin through the Seven Deadly Sins. Write what comes to mind after each prompt. Today: a man who obsessively—and awkwardly—names his envy to the person he's envious of.

MARCH

14

Let's take a spin through the Seven Deadly Sins. Write what comes to mind after each prompt. Today: someone endangered by another person's pride.

15

Beware the Ides of March. If there were a holiday for betrayal (or soothsaying), this would be it. Write about a moment of betrayal in your own life.

MARCH

16

"A writer who
waits for the ideal
conditions under
which to work will
die without putting
a word on paper,"
said E. B. White.
Congratulations
on writing today.
Now go ahead and
describe your ideal
conditions.

Jot down something crazy you've seen a drunk person do, or something audacious (and perhaps ill-advised) you've done under the influence of liquid courage.

18

What does the
phrase "an act of
righteous defiance"
conjure up in
your mind?

A beautiful leather valise is sitting on your bed. You pick up the luggage tag and read: EMOTIONAL BAGGAGE. What's inside?

20

An ekphrastic poem creates a vivid depiction of an artwork, often with the poet amplifying or expanding upon the content of the original piece. This method can be applied to almost any medium, from sculpture to film. See John Keats's "Ode on a Grecian Urn" as a primary example, then attempt your own ekphrasis.

Spring has sprung.
Listen to Antonio
Vivaldi's *Spring* from
The Four Seasons and
write what comes to
mind as you do it.

MARCH

22

In a 1754 letter, Horace Walpole explained his concept of Serendipity, coined from a fairy tale called *The Three Princes of Serendip* (an old name for Sri Lanka), in which the royals were "always making discoveries, by accidents and sagacity, of things which they were not in quest of." Record one of your own experiences of serendipity.

MARCH

23

What does your last name mean? Where does it come from? Imagine the first person who bore this name and write about how he or she got it.

MARCH

24

"A hero ventures forth from the world of common day into a region of supernatural wonder: fabulous forces are there encountered and a decisive victory is won: the hero comes back from this mysterious adventure with the power to bestow boons on his fellow man." —*Joseph Campbell*

Which of your favorite heroes from literature does this describe?

He yelled, "Do not
try and play Ping-
Pong with a manic
depressive!" Write
more dialogue from
this conversation.

26

Shel Silverstein built a whole book upon spoonerisms, in which the beginnings of two words are swapped. *Runny Babbit: A Billy Sook* features Runny, whose parents, Dummy and Mad, often remind him to "shake a tower," or "dash the wishes." Have some fun coming up with amusing spoonerisms of your own.

27

If you could send
a message to any
deceased person,
what would you say
and to whom?

MARCH

28

Think of a time
when you were
disoriented. Perhaps
you were woken up
from sleep, injured,
or jet-lagged in a
foreign country. How
can you translate this
experience into a
more dramatic one?

Write an accelerated story—cram as much action and description as you can into an event that lasts just ten seconds in real time.

_____
_____
_____
_____
_____
_____
_____
_____
_____
_____
_____
_____
_____
_____
_____
_____
_____
_____
_____
_____
_____
_____
_____
_____

MARCH

30

Search the word
peace on Pinterest,
and choose your own
writing adventure
based on something
you find there.

31

Think of a major celebrity, and inhabit that celebrity's mind on a day when they are dying to get a cup of coffee without being recognized.

APRIL

1

Write a few ends
to this joke. "How
many writers does
it take to screw in a
lightbulb? . . ."

APRIL

2

Take a deep breath
and look around
you. Describe your
surroundings in a few
precise sentences.

APRIL

3

Use a repetitive
sound as a central
part of a composition
(e.g., a dripping
faucet, clacking train
tracks, a printer).

If you could leave a
note for yourself to
read this time next
year, what would it
say?

5

If a deceased
relative were to
appear to you as
a bird, what bird
would that person
be and why?

Let out some "purple prose"—an overly florid description— of anything.

7

Think of an activity that has engaged your senses—maybe it's swimming, cooking, or hiking— and write about it without including thought or emotion. Find out what can be conveyed through physicality alone.

Imagine your grandfather as a young man, laughing. What is he up to?

9

Write about
something that
thrills you.

10

_____ is burning. Fill in the place/ thing and the rest of the scene.

APRIL

11

Select a line from
a poem that feels
obtuse or hard to
understand and
make it the first line
of your own poem.
Enjoy the catharsis
that comes from
forcing it to make
sense in a context
under your control.

APRIL

12

"They had an affair."
Does this line pique
your interest, inspire
scorn, or bring on
foreboding? Run with
that emotion.

13

What does wisdom
mean to you?

14

Turn on the radio
and write a few
sentences about how
you feel about what
you hear.

15

Today is the day the *Titanic* slipped below water, at 2:20 in the morning, about two and a half hours after striking an iceberg. Imagine a final interaction between two people somewhere on the ship or in the water.

16

Visit the website postsecret.com and write a response to something you find there.

17

You come home
to find a hyacinth
macaw in your
bathroom. How did
he get there? And
what is he saying?

There are many legends of diabolical delivery systems— think of the Trojan Horse or blankets laden with smallpox. Invent one of your own.

APRIL

19

How do people
sometimes
misunderstand
or misinterpret
you?

_____

_____

_____

_____

_____

_____

_____

_____

_____

_____

_____

_____

_____

_____

_____

_____

_____

_____

_____

_____

_____

_____

_____

_____

_____

Do you have a
childhood memory
based purely on an
old photograph?
What is it and how
"true" do you think
it really is?

21

If your best friend
were to have a
superpower, what
would it be and why?

Have you ever had a story you were dying to write but didn't know how to begin? Start it from the middle, right here.

APRIL

23

"You don't belong here." What does that statement bring up for you?

24

Give descriptive
nicknames to the
first three people
you interacted
with today.

25

What is something
you care about
deeply and wish
more people would
pay attention to?

Think of stories
that use a piece
of artwork as a
character itself (see
Donna Tartt's *The
Goldfinch* or Oscar
Wilde's *The Picture
of Dorian Gray*) to
come up with an
artwork that could
inspire great fiction.
What did you choose
and why?

APRIL

27

Write a vignette
infused with nidor,
the particular scent
of cooking meat or
burning fat.

28

Recall a favorite childhood game (e.g., a board game, a sport, something from the playground) and translate the action/strategy into an adult life.

APRIL

29

"For sale: baby shoes, never worn"—often cited as a prime example of flash fiction—speaks volumes in six words. Try to achieve the same here.

30

Think of the best meal you've ever eaten in terms of the food itself. Think of the best meal you've ever eaten in terms of the place/experience. Think of the best meal you've ever eaten in terms of company. Which one wins out as the most superlative and why?

MAY

1

Write a phrase
over and over to
fill this space,
even if the phrase
is not your own.

2

What might a "feat
of strength" mean
without muscle
involved?

MAY

3

ABC! Write a sentence that begins and ends with the letter *a*. ("Animals came to an oasis in the Sahara.") Continue as such through the alphabet —see how many letters you can fit into the space.

_____

_____

_____

_____

_____

_____

_____

_____

_____

_____

_____

_____

_____

_____

_____

_____

_____

_____

_____

_____

_____

_____

_____

4

Place yourself or
a character in utter
whiteness. What is
happening? What
can be heard,
felt? What kind of
whiteness is it?

MAY

5

The Mexican holiday of Cinco de Mayo celebrates the David and Goliath victory of the Mexican army against occupying French forces in 1862, a major morale booster for the Mexican people. Conjure up an image of Mexico in your mind and describe what you see here.

6

Take the following in
a positive direction:
"There's just
something about . . ."

MAY

7

Allow yourself a fan
fiction moment, and
begin an episode
of a favorite TV
series or a sequel to
a beloved book.

*(Hint: it's helpful to
think of a favorite episode
or character and ask
"What if . . . ?")*

8

In honor of May, the month we celebrate mothers, write a scene in which your mother is a child.

MAY

9

In reality: everybody eats. In fiction: it's an option. But part of the power of food is that it is relatable and therefore a valuable way to draw in a reader. Practice for this writing exercise by first observing someone eating and then creating a short character study.

10

Rip a headline from
the news and without
reading the ensuing
article, invent your
own story to follow.

11

Create a rhyming couplet—two lines in the same meter/ length that complete one thought or action. An example is Shakespeare's "Double, double, toil and trouble; / Fire burn, and cauldron bubble."

Exquisite Corpse #1: In an Exquisite Corpse, writers pass a story back and forth, writing one sentence at a time. Find a friend and write an Exquisite Corpse with them.

13

What's your sign?
Find today's
horoscope and write
about how true or
false it is.

14

If you were to completely change careers or life direction, where would you go and what would you do?

_____

_____

_____

_____

_____

_____

_____

_____

_____

_____

_____

_____

_____

_____

_____

_____

_____

_____

_____

_____

_____

MAY

15

When was the last
time you witnessed
behavior that made
you uncomfortable?
What was happening?

_____

_____

_____

_____

_____

_____

_____

_____

_____

_____

_____

_____

_____

_____

_____

_____

_____

_____

_____

_____

_____

_____

Your phone buzzes
an alert: it's a text
message from an
unknown number.
What does the
text say?

MAY

17

What is a creative
block for you and
how do you
overcome it?

A story exercise:
A woman in a coma
keeps whispering,
"Aster Chriseldis,
Aster Chriseldis."
Who is Aster
Chriseldis?

MAY

19

What was a favorite
book from your
childhood? What
did you enjoy
about it and what
stayed with you?

Write about a
possession that was
prized by you and is
now lost.

MAY

21

A moonglade is the bright reflection of moonlight found on the surface of water. Write a scene where something glides through a moonglade.

22

Think of a person, place, or thing. Now try to describe that noun without adjectives (metaphors are fair play).

MAY

23

What would you
most like to dream
about tonight?
Foretell your
dream here.

What did you dream
about last night?
If you can't recall,
you'll just have to
make up something.

MAY

25

Write what comes
before this phrase:
". . . meanwhile an
asteroid was headed
straight for Earth."

When was the last
time you argued
with someone?
What do you wish
you had said to them
that you didn't?

27

Consider your
favorite outfit or
article of clothing.
Describe it in
detail here.

Although you're obscured from the sun, the air is thick and warm on your bare skin. You cannot hear each other over the deafening rush of water, so you make faces and gestures in the semidarkness, your backs pressed against the rock. What happens next?

MAY

29

Write about
the last time you
truly relaxed.

30

Think about a
time when fear
stopped you from
doing something.
What would have
happened if you
had done it?

MAY

31

What's a book that
you haven't read but
feel that you should?

_____
_____
_____
_____
_____
_____
_____
_____
_____
_____
_____
_____
_____
_____
_____
_____
_____
_____
_____
_____
_____
_____
_____
_____
_____
_____

1

One of Henry Miller's commandments was: "Keep human! See people, go places, drink if you feel like it." So sally forth and be human—and record some dialogue you overhear when you do it.

JUNE

2

Fill in the blanks:
_____ gets under my
skin. I wish I could
_____.

Pick a word at random from a dictionary. How does its definition relate to your day, if at all?

4

What is the worst
that could happen?

5

In six sentences, record your thoughts on a memorable member of your family.

JUNE

6

Recast an ancient
myth in modern
times. Perhaps
Icarus is now a kite-
surfing instructor,
or Narcissus is
a selfie king.

7

Take stock of anything to which you can attach a number. For example: It's been _____ days since I last cried, _____ times I've sworn in front of a child, _____ national parks visited, _____ years since I've had Mountain Dew, etc. Try it out.

JUNE

8

Who do you wish you
could write like?

_____

_____

_____

_____

_____

_____

_____

_____

_____

_____

_____

_____

_____

_____

_____

_____

_____

_____

_____

_____

_____

_____

_____

_____

_____

_____

_____

_____

_____

_____

9

Compose a joke. It could be a knock-knock joke, a variation of the old three-guys-in-a-bar setup ("A butcher, a baker, and a CEO walk into a bar . . ."), or simply a pun.

JUNE

10

When you were
ten years old, you
wrote your deepest
secret on a message
in a bottle. Today,
you open that bottle.
What's inside?

JUNE

11

Describe the kind of person you imagine when reading this line: "She only bought lottery tickets when it was a record-breaking jackpot."

JUNE

12

Exquisite Corpse #2:
In an Exquisite
Corpse, writers pass
a story back and
forth, writing one
sentence at a time.
Find a friend and
write an Exquisite
Corpse with them.

JUNE

13

Let's pretend there's a rapper with these lyrics: "Her callipygian rondure is a Rubenesque rapture." Can you come up with another line from this artist?

JUNE

14

Turn on the
television or a
YouTube video at
random. Record
the first line of
dialogue you hear.
Now continue the
discussion.

15

According to Marcel Proust, "The best vaccine against anger is to watch others in its throes." Recount an anger repellent experience here.

JUNE

16

Use this space to
describe the sky
without using the
words *blue*, *gray*,
green, *clouds*, or *sun*.

17

What else—in addition to "idle hands"—could you call the Devil's playground?

JUNE

18

For mid-June, a time when we celebrate fathers, write a portrait of a father who is the opposite of your own.

_____

_____

_____

_____

_____

_____

_____

_____

_____

_____

_____

_____

_____

_____

_____

_____

_____

_____

_____

_____

_____

_____

_____

19

Describe the last
time you were
awake at dawn.

20

Think of the word *happiness*. Jot down the first ten words that come to mind.

Happy solstice! It is the longest day of the year. Write a few lines—either a description or an emotional response—centered on sunlight.

22

What is something
you used to believe
but no longer do?
How do you feel
when you look back
on that thought
or time?

23

Think about something often overlooked—a floral pattern on a dress, the grain of wood on a table, etc.—and write about it here.

_____

_____

_____

_____

_____

_____

_____

_____

_____

_____

_____

_____

_____

_____

_____

_____

_____

_____

_____

_____

_____

_____

_____

_____

JUNE

24

Picture the most
beautiful place
you've ever
experienced and
detail it here.

Are you a giver or a receiver? Write about a generous act and the impact it had on the giver or the beneficiary.

26

Imagine you were
born in a different
country. How
different would
your life be?

Come up with a
wedding toast for
someone you love in
a platonic way.

28

A time machine drops you into the passenger seat of a silver Porsche convertible speeding along a California road. You notice the dash looks vintage, then you notice the driver: James Dean. He turns his head and smiles at you while shifting into high gear. What do you do next?

29

What is a line—from
a novel, film, TV
show, etc.—that has
stayed with you over
time, and why do you
think that is?

JUNE

30

You're in a public
bathroom when the
lights go out. What
happens next?

1

Jack Kerouac advised writers: "Like Proust, be an old teahead of time." Create a similar turn of phrase by filling in the blanks: Like _____, be a(n) _____ of _____.

JULY

2

It's July 2, the midpoint of the year. Has writing become autotelic for you? Are you writing for its intrinsic value rather than external reward? Are you finding pleasure in the act more so than the result?

JULY

3

What is a mundane task you enjoy doing? Washing dishes? Dusting? Walking the dog? Write with reverence about whatever act it is, and elevate it to something sublime, holy, or profound.

JULY

4

Celebrate a moment
of your own
independence here.

If a stranger was to describe your hair, what would he or she say?

6

Is there a moment
from your past
that you wish you
could change?

7

Is there something
you covet or hope
to buy? Think of
this object of desire
and personify it.
How would this
person dress, talk,
move? What kind of
relationship would
you have with it?

JULY

8

In the 1950s and '60s William S. Burroughs popularized the "cut-up" technique, later employed by lyricists like David Bowie. In a 2008 interview, Bowie explained: "You write down a paragraph or two describing different subjects, creating a kind of 'story ingredients' list, I suppose, and then cut the sentences into four- or five-word sections, mix 'em up, and reconnect them." Use two previous entries as your material for a cut-up.

Describe in detail the
most recent person
you've met.

10

Imagine your sworn
enemy (fictional
or otherwise).
What complimentary
things would he
or she have to
say about you?

What is a
nonphysical trait
you find especially
attractive, and when
was the last time
you experienced its
allure?

JULY

12

Think about your
state of mind exactly
one year ago. Write
about it here.

What are "victory arms"? Think of Michael Phelps after winning any of his twenty-two Olympic medals or marathon runners crossing the finish line, arms in the air, whether they've won or not. Turns out the posture is not a *V* for victory, but an innate behavior, performed even by Paralympic athletes who were blind from birth. Channel that feeling of triumph for some kind of fictional climactic moment, athletic or otherwise.

JULY

14

Bastille Day gives us a reason to reflect on the French Revolution and the repeating history of people shedding blood for their ideals. Is there a historical event or a great personal sacrifice that stirs you to write about it?

Choose two random nouns, two adjectives, and two verbs. Got them? Now write something with all six.

JULY

16

Clear your mind.
Write a sentence as
quickly as you can
without overthinking.

_____
_____
_____
_____
_____
_____
_____
_____
_____
_____
_____
_____
_____
_____
_____
_____
_____
_____
_____
_____
_____
_____
_____
_____
_____

While clichés
in writing should
generally be avoided
like the plague, they
can also be useful for
creating seamless,
natural dialogue.
Test it out.

18

Attempt to inhabit a character very different from yourself. Perhaps he or she is monastic, or of an extreme political persuasion, or maybe the individual is cruel, conniving, or even depraved. Put yourself in this person's shoes, and write what he or she is thinking at this moment.

Write a list of the ten
things that you need
to be creative.

20

What makes a good
friend, and how did/
do you become one?
Did/do you have a
role model?

JULY

21

A griffin is a beast with the head and wings of an eagle and the body of a lion. Think up your own combination of animals to create a fantastic monster. What is it called?

JULY

22

Exquisite Corpse #3:
In an Exquisite
Corpse, writers pass
a story back and
forth, writing one
sentence at a time.
Find a friend and
write an Exquisite
Corpse with them.

JULY

23

Do you seek conflict
or avoid it? Write
about an exception
to your rule.

JULY

24

What is your hunch
or paranoia about
how you will die? Or
how do you die in
dreams?

JULY

25

Imagine a phone conversation between two close friends. What are they talking about? Write their dialogue here.

JULY

26

Eavesdropping doesn't have to mean leaving your house. Visit overheard everywhere.com for inspirational dialogue. Try to weave two previously unconnected conversations into a single discussion.

What is your
personal anthem,
and what makes you
choose that song?

28

Think of two of your favorite films. Can you write a plot synopsis of each in just one sentence?

_____

_____

_____

_____

_____

_____

_____

_____

_____

_____

_____

_____

_____

_____

_____

_____

_____

_____

_____

_____

_____

_____

_____

_____

Have you ever
thought a person was
a sociopath—or a
psychopath? What
made you think so,
and how did they
make you feel?
Finally, how could
you adopt some
of their traits and
behaviors to create a
villain for a story?

JULY

30

Just as splinters
work their way to
the surface of our
skin, given time,
stones work their
way to the topsoil
over successive
frosts. What themes
or ideas "surface" in
your writing?

Maya Angelou dedicated *I Know Why the Caged Bird Sings* to: "MY SON, GUY JOHNSON, AND ALL THE STRONG BLACK BIRDS OF PROMISE who defy the odds and gods and sing their songs." It is a dedication hard to beat, but perhaps it can inspire one of your own. Who would you dedicate a book to and what would it say?

AUGUST

1

The wine world is full of fantastic takes on aroma, from the sublime to surprising (see tasting notes about cut green grass or asphalt on a summer's day). Try to immerse yourself in the bouquet and taste of wine—or cheese, or coffee—and let the descriptions flow, no matter how wacky they get.

2

Are you at a point
where you feel
you could write a
meaningful memoir?
Why or why not?
If you were to do
it, what cover copy
would you give it?

AUGUST

3

In a few sentences,
describe the most
dishonest person
you've ever met.

4

Can you describe the
pain of loneliness?
What does it sound
like? What does it
look like?

AUGUST

5

Think of an accent
you find appealing.
What makes it
seductive and how
can you describe
its allure?

If you could have
a "do-over" of any
kind, what would
you use it for and
what would you do
differently this time?

AUGUST

7

If you could spend a
day with one writer,
living or dead, who
would it be and why?

Think of where you grew up and try to bring out elements of regionalism that could be used in a story. An example might be a tale set in the Ozarks, where the grandma is happy to use the blinky milk to make biscuits.

AUGUST

9

Take up the spirit
of confessional
literature and try to
unburden yourself
of something you're
not proud.

10

What is the smallest room/space in your home? Can you create a story set in just this place?

AUGUST

11

Think of a major
city. Now think of
a decade between
1850 and 1950.
Now do a Google
Images search of
that place at that
time. What photo
grabs you? Let it
spark today's entry.

When you think
of the term
unconditional love,
what comes to mind?
Try to be as brief
as possible in your
answer.

To which fairy tale do you feel connected? The creepiness of "Little Red Riding Hood" or the magic of "Cinderella"? What makes it special to you?

14

When did you last
want to celebrate
being right about
something? Or do
you currently feel
"in the right" about
some matter? Write
it out.

AUGUST

15

Anaïs Nin said: "It is the function of art to renew our perception. What we are familiar with we cease to see. The writer shakes up the familiar scene, and, as if by magic, we see a new meaning in it." How does this statement relate to your writing goals?

16

Think of five different products from five different sections of the grocery store. Now visualize them together at the checkout. Who do you see standing there, buying this assortment of stuff? Describe the person in any way you please.

AUGUST

17

There is an
unmarked manila
envelope waiting for
you in your mailbox.
What is in it?

18

Outline a compelling cliff-hanger, something that leaves a big dangling question for readers. Be sure to build up tension to give your cliff-hanger dizzying height, for the reader to fall farther back into the story.

19

If you could
broadcast a thirty-
second message to
the entire world—
over seven billion
people—what would
you say?

Does reading the phrase "the red wheelbarrow" immediately conjure up William Carlos Williams's poem of the same name? Williams was one of the imagists, early modern poets who focused on an economy of language in free verse that spoke as much in image as in rhythm. Try it for yourself in a short, visually focused poem.

AUGUST

21

Describe a beloved
toy from childhood.

22

Go to the edge of a bookshelf, count seven books in, and take that one out. Open it to page seven and count to the seventh sentence on that page. Write a poem that starts with something from that sentence.

AUGUST

23

Attempt to recall
a bad date or a
botched interview,
or any one-on-
one situation that
went awry with
awkwardness. What
stands out to you?

24

Describe your
feelings about sleep.

AUGUST

25

In *Neuromancer*, William Gibson writes, "The sky above the port was the color of television, tuned to a dead channel." Try to create a description—as evocative as the one above—about the current sky.

26

Fill this space with
a list of people and
things that you are
grateful for.

AUGUST

27

Do you have a
handbag, a backpack,
a briefcase? Describe
the receptacle
and all of its current
contents.

Conduct a field study of your local neighborhood. If you were new to the area, what would be the three things that would stand out to you?

AUGUST

29

Describe the texture of an everyday object. It could be the coarseness of denim or the cool smoothness of a pebble.

In a few sentences,
describe your
breakfast routine.

AUGUST

31

Continue this thought:
"I remember . . ."

1

Respond to this quote from Junot Díaz in any manner you please: "In order to write the book you want to write, in the end you have to become the person you need to become to write that book."

SEPTEMBER

2

Are you a sports fan?
If so, what draws you
to a particular sport?
If not, what repels
you about the sports
world?

3

When you reach the age of one hundred and have lived the life of your dreams, what would you title your autobiography? (Feel free to add a subtitle, too.)

SEPTEMBER

4

When was the last
time you held a baby,
and how did it make
you feel?

5

What do you think
about the idea of
soul mates?

SEPTEMBER

6

As an exercise
in examining
transference (when
an object takes on
more importance
than it should), think
of an object and
run with whatever
first comes to mind.
Describe what
you see. There's
no need to explain
why you chose it,
just get the thing
nailed down. Then
continue writing all
the emotions that the
image "tells" you.

There is something
strange on top of
your roof right now.
What is it?

_____

_____

_____

_____

_____

_____

_____

_____

_____

_____

_____

_____

_____

_____

_____

_____

_____

_____

_____

_____

_____

_____

_____

_____

_____

_____

_____

_____

SEPTEMBER

8

If you could be
physically present
for any event
in the past or the
future, what would it
be and why?

Use some kind of unique flora—it could be a Joshua tree, a bird of paradise, a redwood, a Venus flytrap, etc.—as an essential element in a short piece.

SEPTEMBER

10

If your spouse, partner, or hypothetical lover were to have a single one-night stand yet never communicate with or see that person ever again, would it be better to know or not to know that it had happened? Why?

11

Write an "in memoriam" to someone, something, or even a way of living or thinking you've lost or let go.

SEPTEMBER

12

Complete this
sentence (as yourself
or someone else):
"I can't help staring
when . . ."

13

Write about a
diapason—a deep,
melodic outpouring
of sound, such as a
chorus of bullfrogs.

SEPTEMBER

14

Let out a stream
of consciousness.
The only rule is that
you keep your pen
moving.

15

In her diary, Virginia Woolf once wrote: "I've shirked two parties, and another Frenchman, and buying a hat, and tea with Hilda Trevelyan, for I really can't combine all this with keeping all my imaginary people going." Purge some of your small disruptions here.

SEPTEMBER

16

When was
the last time you
slept outside, and
how did it feel?

17

Imagine a
refrigerator full to
the brim with good
stuff to eat. List
what is inside.

SEPTEMBER

18

Look around you to find a visual pattern—in bricks, in a bedspread, in flowers—and write a short piece based on the design.

Say you were to
make a break with
your past, what
might this mean for
you?

_____

_____

_____

_____

_____

_____

_____

_____

_____

_____

_____

_____

_____

_____

_____

_____

_____

_____

_____

_____

_____

_____

_____

20

A story begins,
"'I won it for you,'
he said, placing the
object in her hands.
As she received it,
her elbows swung
back and her hands
dipped to her waist,
its weight a startling
surprise . . ." what
happens next?

You're at a late-night poker game. Where is it? Who are you playing against? Are you winning or losing?

SEPTEMBER

22

Equinox means a
time of equal day
and night. Create a
story concept around
this balance.

23

Madeleine L'Engle once said, "You have to write the book that wants to be written. And if the book will be too difficult for grown-ups, then you write it for children." If you were to write a young adult or children's book, how might it start?

SEPTEMBER

24

At a raucous house
party, one woman
stands alone near an
open window with
a smirk on her face.
What's her story?

25

If you were given
the chance to ask
any one person a
question, knowing he
or she could tell only
the truth in reply,
what would you ask
of whom?

SEPTEMBER

26

Exquisite Corpse #4:
In an Exquisite
Corpse, writers
pass a story back
and forth, writing
one sentence at
a time. Find a
friend and write an
Exquisite Corpse
with them.

Visit
humansofnewyork.com,
choose a person,
imagine his or her
home, and write about
it here.

SEPTEMBER

28

Who—or what—has
been your greatest
teacher and why?

29

Imagine shaking hands with any United States President, living or dead, past or future. What does his (or her) handshake feel like?

SEPTEMBER

30

How have you used
your intuition in
the past? Does it
manifest more in the
form of knowledge/
feelings about other
people, yourself, or
nonpersonal events?

_____

_____

_____

_____

_____

_____

_____

_____

_____

_____

_____

_____

_____

_____

_____

_____

_____

_____

_____

_____

_____

_____

_____

_____

1

Steven Brust wrote: "Because here's the thing: No matter how much one tells stories of magical beasts or impossible worlds, in the end, it is always the world of here and now one is writing about. The better one understands that world, the more powerful the stories will be." Write about your here and now to prepare for fantasy worlds in the future.

OCTOBER

2

What associations
does the word
fertility bring
up for you?

3

Peruse jobstr.com, a site where you can ask real people questions about their work. Poke around until you find inspiration, and maybe even ask something of a private eye, a football official, or a forensic scientist. Record it here.

OCTOBER

4

Do you know
the old saw about
dogs and their
owners? Think up a
dog and create an
owner to match.

5

What is your strongest personal quality? Do you find this question hard to answer? Why?

OCTOBER

6

Think of a susurrus sound (such as a whisper or the gentle rustle of curtains or palm fronds in a breeze). Free write about that sound here.

7

According to Christopher Booker, there are only seven plots: tragedy, comedy, overcoming the monster, voyage and return, quest, rags to riches, and rebirth. Try to list a book or a film that fits into each category.

8

Walking along
a deserted street,
you notice writing
carved into the
cement. What
does it say?

Complete this thought: "The greatest tragedy is . . ."

OCTOBER

10

How do you make
someone else's life
better this week?

Take a stab at
finishing these half-
written proverbs:
"One need not devour
a whole chicken to . . ."
(China). "A smiling
face is half the . . ."
(Latvia). "A full cabin
is better than . . ."
(Ireland). "He who
builds according
to everyone's
advice . . ."
(Netherlands). "An
ignorant person is
simply . . ." (Syria).

OCTOBER

12

Can you grin and bear it? Look back on an embarrassing memory and try to retell it with humor.

13

Think about the
littoral, the part of
a beach exposed
only at low tide. As
the tide goes out,
what objects do you
discover?

14

What is a theme
that often comes up
in your writing and
where do you think
it is born from?

15

D. H. Lawrence once said, "I like to write when I feel spiteful. It is like having a good sneeze." Write about a time you felt spiteful.

If you could
personify your
relationship
to money as a
relationship with a
romantic partner,
what would that
be like?

Think about a
familiar place in
your day-to-day
existence. If it
happened to be
haunted, what kind
of ghost would
inhabit this space?

18

"You have a great need for other people to like and admire you, which may be the root of the critical thoughts you have about yourself. Some of your aspirations are unrealistic, but confidence in your untapped potential means you won't give up on your dreams just yet." This is an example of a Barnum Statement (named after P.T.), which is vague and general enough to apply to most people. Try writing one yourself.

If you were to write a story about today's zeitgeist, what would be its central conceit?

OCTOBER

20

In either a movie or
a real-life wedding
ceremony, you've
likely heard this
line: "Should anyone
here present know
of any reason that
this couple should
not be joined in holy
matrimony, speak
now or forever
hold your peace."
Sometimes it's almost
disappointing when
nothing happens at
that would-be climax.
Rather than arresting
a real-life wedding,
do it here instead.

21

The Germans have a name for the feeling of solitude that only comes from being alone in the woods: *Waldeinsamkeit.* What does *Waldeinsamkeit* feel like for you?

OCTOBER

22

Write about a
narcissist you know.
Maybe it's yourself?

OCTOBER

23

Can you recall a memorable birthday celebration—yours or someone else's? What was at the heart of making it great?

OCTOBER

24

"There was a boy called Eustace Clarence Scrubb, and he almost deserved it," wrote C. S. Lewis in *The Voyage of the Dawn Treader.* Start a name bank to draw upon when you need a new character. Try to fill this space with first and last names that are evocative for you. Baby name generators and phone directories can help if you get stuck.

Do you think anyone can become a writer, or is there an essential quality of thinking, reflection, or something else that is innate in people who are talented writers? Has writing always—to some degree—come naturally to you?

26

"Speaking in tongues"
is the fluid vocalizing
of speech-like
syllables that don't
communicate shared
meaning, although
some regard it as a
divine language that's
known only to the
speaker. How could
you write a scene
with glossolalia? How
would you describe it?

27

You've probably heard of the cheeky tradition of adding "in bed" to the end of any fortune cookie text (usually to an amusing result, such as: "In life, your first and last true love is self-love . . . in bed."). Here, we're going to add "in bed" to any literary character of your choosing. What is _____ like . . . in bed?

OCTOBER

28

Sometimes the truth
is indeed stranger
than fiction. What
is the strangest,
most coincidental,
or hardest to explain
thing that's happened
to you or a friend?
Write it out.

29

"The Proustian
memory effect"
describes the
phenomenon of
scent triggering a
flood of memories,
so named for the
evocative description
of madeleine
biscuits tied to
Proust's childhood
in *Remembrance of
Things Past*. (Look
up the passage
on madeleines
for inspiration.)
Which scent has
done this for you?
Or work backward,
thinking of childhood
memories and trying
to conjure scents
with them.

30

What kind of
associations do you
have with the word
activist? Do those
associations change
whether the person
is male or female?
Black or white?

31

As morbid as it may sound, the universality of death lends itself to great literature. To wit, in 2011, all thirteen novels nominated for the Booker Prize shared a death-related plotline. Your task today: write a death scene.

NOVEMBER

1

Give a character
immortal life. What
are his or her main
struggles?

_____

_____

_____

_____

_____

_____

_____

_____

_____

_____

_____

_____

_____

_____

_____

_____

_____

_____

_____

_____

_____

_____

_____

_____

_____

_____

2

Choose an artwork from which you can spin a story. If you need inspiration, check out *I Saw the Figure 5 in Gold* by Charles Demuth, or *Christina's World* by Andrew Wyeth, or *The Wounded Deer* by Frida Kahlo.

3

For his book *In Cold Blood*, Truman Capote could have written, "Nothing of note had ever happened there." Instead he wrote, "Like the waters of the river, like the motorists on the highway, and like the yellow trains streaking down the Santa Fe tracks, drama, in the shape of exceptional happenings, had never stopped there." Try to "Capote" a simple concept in a single sentence by creating an extended simile as he has done here.

NOVEMBER

Do pets have inner
lives? Imagine a
cat or a dog or
another pet, and
tell us what they
are thinking about.

NOVEMBER

5

Imagine a waiting
area of some sort.
There is a person
there, fidgeting. Give
this person a reason
for his or her anxiety,
but in writing the
descriptive scene,
leave out the reason
and see if it comes
through anyway.

6

Research is often a crucial part of writing. Look up something you're curious about, or use Wikipedia's "random article" button until you come across something of interest. Write a brief summary of what you've discovered.

NOVEMBER

7

Can you think of a colloquialism that represents the informal language of a particular place and use it as dialogue? For example, a character from Down East Maine might say, "Just because a cat has her kittens in the oven don't make them biscuits; she might have lived here ten years but she'll always be from away."

8

Take a God's-eye
view to describe
yourself without
using your name,
physical qualities,
or attributes
assigned to you
by family/friends/
society. Who are
you deep down?

NOVEMBER

9

It's time to judge a
book by its cover.
Pull a favorite novel
from your shelf and
take in the cover
design at face value.
How would you
imagine the story
based solely on this
impression?

If you were to write
a blog devoted to a
single esoteric topic,
what would it be?
Create a sample
post here.

NOVEMBER

11

Record a story from
a veteran you know
or have heard about.

12

Write about a
chance encounter
between two
strangers.

NOVEMBER

13

Find a friend's
status update on
social media. Now
build a brief story
off that status.

14

A fight is taking place in the kitchen. Describe everything but the people.

NOVEMBER
15

Sylvia Plath said, "Everything in life is writable about if you have the outgoing guts to do it, and the imagination to improvise. The worst enemy to creativity is self-doubt." Write a positive affirmation for yourself today.

What was the subject and context of your last rant? If you're not much of a ranter, when was the last time you made someone else really laugh?

17

You have a terrible
taste in your mouth.
What's it from?

If you had your pick between writing a feature article for *GQ, The Atlantic, National Geographic,* or *Wired,* which magazine would you choose and what would your piece investigate?

19

Think of a route you often travel. Now describe the journey only through sound. If it helps, pretend as though you're blindfolded in a friend's car, or if a kidnapping scenario is more motivating, imagine that.

What have you done in the name of love? Something rash, silly, or bold? Or have you not but wished you had?

NOVEMBER

21

Write a six-word
memoir for yourself
or someone else.

Finish this sentence:
"You don't know
how difficult it was
when . . ."

NOVEMBER

23

Groucho Marx was
a one-liner king,
giving us such gems
as "I never forget
a face, but in your
case I'll be glad to
make an exception"
and "I don't want to
belong to any club
that will have me as
a member." Try
out your own
one-liner here.

What time of day
are you most
productive and what
conditions or rituals
seem to help?

NOVEMBER

25

Say you come into
a considerable
sum of money.
What is something
extravagant you
would do for
someone else?
Would you do this
type of thing only
for friends and
family, or would
you extend the act
to strangers?

Write about a time
you felt ashamed—
whether or not the
feeling was justified.

27

Describe a person through the marginalia of their life, either the kinds of notes they leave in novels or details from the edges of their life, like where they leave their keys at night or what their fridge or medicine cabinet looks like.

28

Think of a simple, physical act—throwing a ball against a wall, dropping a ceramic plate to the ground, etc. Now describe that act and its consequences in detail.

29

What kind of op-ed
could you submit to
your local paper?

*(Hint: it helps to
pick a topic that you
either know a lot about
or have a personal
relationship with.)*

Use the phrase "see no evil, hear no evil, speak no evil" as the jumping off point for a confession.

DECEMBER

1

What is something
you tend to
notice that others
(probably) don't?

2

Do you have a bio at the ready? Attempt to write or update your bio here (while picturing it on a book jacket, a speaker program, or after a blog post). As an extra challenge, try to add one note of humor to it.

DECEMBER

3

Exquisite Corpse #5:
In an Exquisite
Corpse, writers pass
a story back and
forth, writing one
sentence at a time.
Find a friend and
write an Exquisite
Corpse with them.

DECEMBER

4

As the holiday season approaches, think back on a beloved gift from childhood—and write about it here.

DECEMBER

5

Describe falling
in love as a
resurrection.

If humans
successfully
colonized Mars—
say the outpost had
been up and running
well for a year—
and you were given
the opportunity to
go, would you take
it? Even if it was
a one-way ticket?
Write through
your decision and
what you imagine
it would be like
to give up life on
Earth.

DECEMBER

7

What stimulates you?

Bedridden with cerebral meningitis in a cheap residential hotel in Paris, Oscar Wilde said, "This wallpaper and I are fighting a duel to the death. Either it goes or I do." He died a few weeks later. Use this milieu as inspiration for a description of an invalid's room, perhaps even Wilde's own.

DECEMBER

9

Write about a race
that begins and ends
in this small space.

If you had to describe a place as your spiritual home, or a group of people as your spiritual family, what/who would that be and why?

DECEMBER

11

Open a random
book to a random,
right-hand page.
Read the last
sentence and write
what you imagine
could come next.
(Yes, you can look
at the real outcome
in the book after
you're done.)

Recall a time of visceral fear. How would you describe the experience only through sensation rather than your thoughts, emotions, or the event itself?

DECEMBER

13

In the film, *American Beauty*, one teenager shows another video footage he's taken of a plastic bag dancing in a breeze against brick and concrete, saying, "It's hard to stay mad when there's so much beauty in the world." Can you devise a scene in which something ugly or mundane suddenly makes an emotional impact?

Describe a first: a
first kiss, first pet,
first dance—yours or
someone else's.

DECEMBER

15

Listen to Louis
L'Amour, who said,
"A writer's brain
is like a magician's
hat. If you're going
to get anything out
of it, you have to put
something in it first."
Simply copy down a
piece of writing that
you love here.

Peel the personality of someone you know like an onion. There is the protective exterior—what they present to the world—and then there are layers and layers until you come to the heart. See how far you can go.

17

Pen in hand, a man stares down at a contract, sighs, and signs the document. What is the contract for?

How do you feel about your educational history and who you have been as a student? Do these things affect you today?

19

Do you think
the Internet is a
reflection of society
or its own kind of
society? Will the
Internet ultimately
prove to be a force
for good or evil?

Charles Dickens was described by a friend as having "a hankering after ghosts." He didn't just write about them, he hunted them as part of London's Ghost Club in the mid-1800s. Do you have a good ghost story to share? If not, write one about Dickens on the hunt.

21

Write a scene that embodies *hygge*. *Hygge* is a Danish concept that conveys the emotional coziness of conviviality. Fire and candlelight are often used to create an atmosphere ripe for *hygge*.

In his memoir, *On Writing,* Stephen King implores, "Kill your darlings, kill your darlings, even when it breaks your egocentric little scribbler's heart, kill your darlings." Find a previous entry you quite liked and rewrite it.

DECEMBER

23

What will change
in ten years?

From the Department of Good News for Visionary People, a quote from Julian Barnes (in *Flaubert's Parrot*): "Happiness lies in the imagination, not the act. Pleasure is found first in anticipation, later in memory." Studies have shown that the reality of gratification can pale in comparison to planning, imagining, and remembering. Use this space to plan an adventure.

DECEMBER

25

If you had the
power to decree a
new holiday, what
would it honor?
How would we
celebrate it? What
would some of the
essentials of this
holiday be, and
what foods would be
associated with it?

26

Write a "conversation" without spoken words.

(A hint if you need it: body language.)

DECEMBER

27

Describe your
best feature.

In Cassandra Clare's *Clockwork Angel*, Tessa warns that you must be careful of books "and what is inside them, for words have the power to change us." Write about a book that has changed you.

DECEMBER

29

As the year comes to
a close, think about
your creative goals.
What do you want
for next year?